Protecting
Our Planet

What Can We Do About OZONE LOSS?

David J. Jakubiak

PowerKiDS
press.

New York

For Sallie Wolf, Pamela Todd, Janet Nolan, Patti Cone, and Judy Dooley—amazing writers and friends

Published in 2012 by The Rosen Publishing Group, Inc.
29 East 21st Street, New York, NY 10010

First Edition

Editor: Amelie von Zumbusch
Book Design: Kate Laczynski
Layout Design: Julio Gil

Photo Credits: Cover (main) Grant Faint/Workbook Stock/Getty Images; cover (inset), p. 12 (inset) Newsmakers/Getty Images; pp. 4, 6, 12 (main), 14, 16, 18, 20 Shutterstock.com; p. 8 iStockphoto/Thinkstock; p. 10 Guy Clavel/AFP/Getty Images.

Library of Congress Cataloging-in-Publication Data

Jakubiak, David J.
 What can we do about ozone loss? / by David J. Jakubiak. — 1st ed.
     p. cm. — (Protecting our planet)
 Includes index.
 ISBN 978-1-4488-4985-7 (library binding) — ISBN 978-1-4488-5118-8 (pbk.) —
 ISBN 978-1-4488-5379-3 (6-pack)
 1. Ozone-depleting substances—Juvenile literature. 2. Pollution prevention—Juvenile literature.
 3. Ozone layer depletion—Juvenile literature. I. Title.
 TD887.O95J355 2012
 363.738'75—dc22

2011000156

Manufactured in the United States of America

CPSIA Compliance Information: Batch #WS11PK: For Further Information contact Rosen Publishing, New York, New York at 1-800-237-9932

CONTENTS

A baseball cap helps keep your eyes safe from some of the Sun's rays. The ozone layer does this, too!

Earth's Sunscreen

Earth's plants and animals depend on the Sun. They need its light and warmth to live and grow. Too much sunlight can hurt plants and animals, though. Luckily, a layer of gases called the **ozone layer** surrounds Earth. The ozone layer acts as Earth's sunscreen. It keeps some of the Sun's rays from reaching Earth.

Pollution is causing problems in the ozone layer. Every spring, a hole forms in the ozone layer over Antarctica because of pollution. Pollution has also made the ozone layer thinner around the world.

Many countries are working together to fix the problems with the ozone layer. Their work seems to be helping. However, there is still much work to be done.

While most ozone is in the ozone layer, there is some in every layer of the atmosphere. Near Earth, ozone makes it hard to see through air.

From Oxygen to Ozone

Earth's ozone layer is one of many layers of gases around Earth. Together, these layers make up Earth's **atmosphere**. The atmosphere's bottom layer is the air we breathe.

The ozone layer got its name because it has the atmosphere's highest **ozone** levels. Ozone is a gas that forms from another gas called **oxygen**. The Sun's heat turns some oxygen in the atmosphere into ozone.

Most of the oxygen in the atmosphere comes from plants. Plants make oxygen and release it into the atmosphere. Earth did not always have an ozone layer. The oxygen and ozone in the atmosphere have built up over billions of years.

DID YOU KNOW?

Ozone is also made when sunlight hits pollution from cars, factories, and fires. This ozone hangs close to Earth and makes the air hard to breathe.

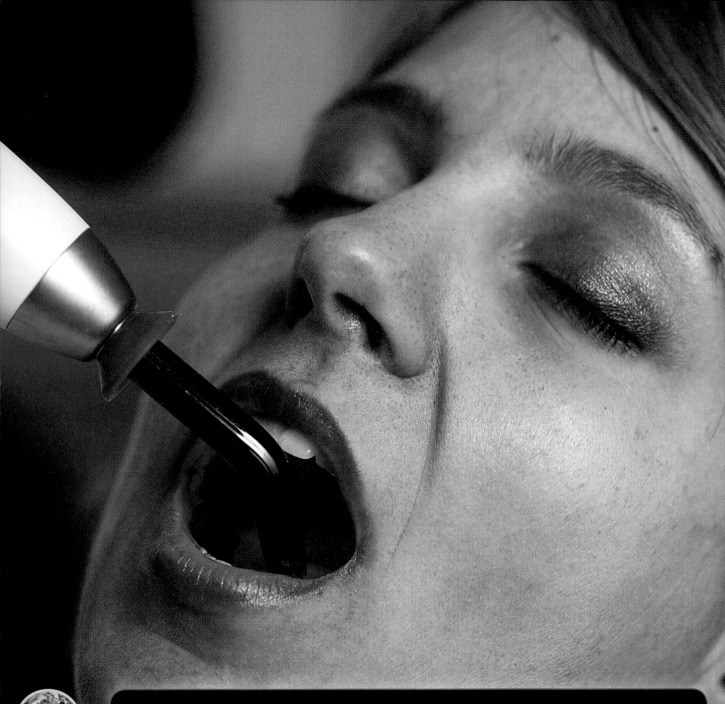

Too much ultraviolet light is harmful. Ultraviolet rays can also be useful, though. Dentists use ultraviolet light to kill germs.

A Blanket of Protection

The ozone layer blocks some of the Sun's rays. The energy that comes from the Sun takes many forms. One form is a ray of light you can see. Another form is an **ultraviolet ray**. The ozone layer is very good at blocking ultraviolet rays. In fact, it blocks between 97 and 99 percent of ultraviolet rays that come from the Sun.

Ultraviolet rays can hurt all living things, from palm trees to people. The ozone layer forms a blanket around Earth about 6 to 10 miles (10–16 km) above the ground. Before the ozone layer formed, the Sun's ultraviolet rays made it impossible for anything to live on Earth's surface. In those days, things could live only in the oceans.

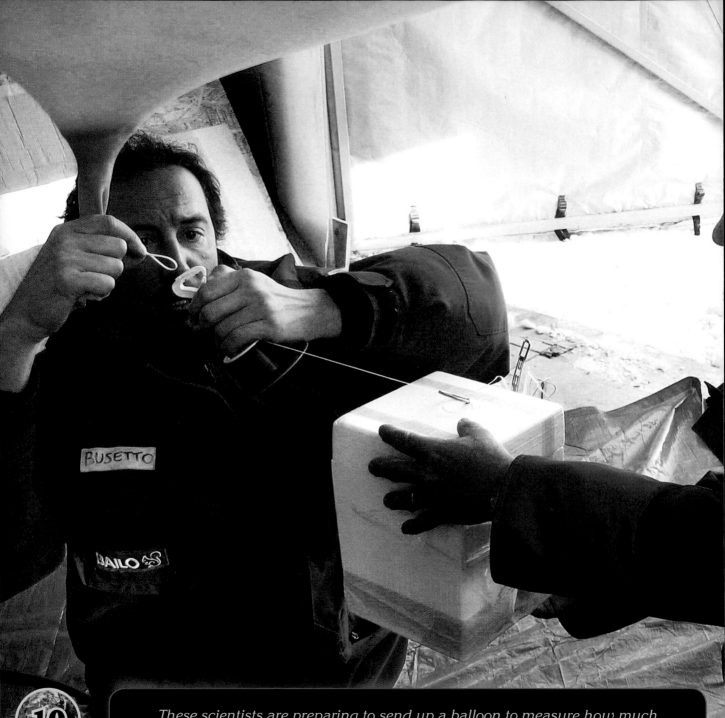

These scientists are preparing to send up a balloon to measure how much ozone there is in a certain layer of the atmosphere.

Since the ozone layer is so important to life on Earth, scientists keep a close eye on it. They take measurements of the ozone layer every day from all over the world. Scientists often use machines fixed to airplanes or hanging from balloons to take those measurements. Scientists keep track of how much ozone they find. They also note the amount of other gases found in the ozone layer.

Scientists watch the ozone layer from above and below, too. They use information from **satellites** to measure how many ultraviolet rays the ozone layer is blocking. Satellites are things that people send up into the sky to circle Earth. On the ground, scientists use the information from satellites to measure how many ultraviolet rays are reaching Earth.

Antarctica is Earth's coldest place. Inset: *In 2000, scientists made this picture of the Antarctic ozone hole as it was in September of that year.*

Big Trouble

In the 1980s, scientists measuring the ozone layer made a scary discovery. There was a hole in the ozone layer over Antarctica during the springtime. The ozone layer did not disappear inside the hole, but it was so thin that it let in lots of ultraviolet rays.

Scientists knew that pollution was thinning the ozone layer all over the world. However, they now discovered that the very cold temperatures in Antarctica made ozone disappear even faster there. Scientists also noted that ozone levels were low on the other side of the world, over the Arctic. However, there was no hole there. This is likely because Antarctica is even colder than the Arctic.

CFCs were used in spray paint cans, like the ones these boys are using. The CFCs made the paint spray out more easily.

Ozone Eaters

People caused the problems with the ozone layer by mistake. No one knew it, but some **chemicals** commonly used in the twentieth century destroy ozone. Chemicals are kinds of matter that can cause other matter to change. People use chemicals to do all sorts of jobs. The chemicals that were destroying the ozone layer were **chlorofluorocarbons**, or CFCs. CFCs were used to keep refrigerators cool and to help **aerosol**, or spray, cans work better.

When CFCs were released in the air, they floated up to the ozone layer. There, they broke down and formed a gas called **chlorine**. Chlorine destroyed ozone faster than new ozone could be made.

Wear sunglasses to keep your eyes safe from ultraviolet light. Try to get sunglasses that block 100 percent of ultraviolet rays.

When the ozone hole appears each spring, twice as many ultraviolet rays reach Antarctica. The ozone layer over the rest of Earth is getting thinner, too. More ultraviolet rays are slipping through in many places.

Too much ultraviolet light can make it hard for plants to grow. Fish, shrimp, crab, and frog eggs may not hatch if they get too much ultraviolet light. Ultraviolet rays are also a danger to people. They hurt people's eyes. They also cause sunburns. Sunburns are painful. They also cause lasting harm to skin **cells**. Cells are small parts that make up living things. If their skin cells are damaged enough, people can get a sickness called **skin cancer**.

DID YOU KNOW?

People are not the only animals getting sunburned because of problems with the ozone layer. Scientists have found that more whales are getting sunburns, too.

18

Refrigerators once used CFCs and HCFCs. Happily, today's refrigerators no longer use these chemicals.

Stopping the Ozone Eaters

People around the world are working together to save the ozone layer. In 1987, leaders from the United States and other countries signed an agreement called the Montreal Protocol. The countries promised to reduce the amount of CFCs they used. In time, they would stop using them at all. The Montreal Protocol has been updated several times. Almost 200 countries have signed on to it.

In place of CFCs, many countries started using gases called hydrochlorofluorocarbons, or HCFCs, and hydrofluorocarbons, or HFCs. HCFCs and HFCs are better for the ozone layer but still hurt the **environment**. Countries must stop using HCFCs by 2030.

DID YOU KNOW?

Many countries stopped using CFCs in the 1990s. However, these chemicals can stick around for many years. In fact, scientists expect the ozone layer to have reached its thinnest point in 2010.

The ozone layer makes it safe for kids to play outside. People everywhere hope that efforts to stop ozone loss will work.

Rays of Hope

Today, scientists are already seeing signs that efforts to save the ozone layer are working. They are finding smaller amounts of CFCs and other chemicals that hurt the ozone layer in the atmosphere.

In 2006, the hole in the ozone layer over Antarctica was the largest it had ever been. It was about twice the size of Antarctica itself. However, the hole has gotten smaller since then. If countries keep working together, scientists think that the ozone layer could get back to the thickness it was in 1980 by 2065. The Montreal Protocol has been a big success. This success shows us that people's efforts really can help solve environmental problems.

Helping Out and Staying Safe

You can help stop ozone loss. Understanding the problem is the first step. Learn everything you can about the ozone layer. Follow the latest news about it. Talk to your friends, teachers, and family about the ozone layer, too.

Until the problems with the ozone layer are fixed, people around the world need to keep themselves safe from ultraviolet rays. Try to stay out of the sun between 10 o'clock a.m. and 4 o'clock p.m. When you are in the sun, remember to wear sunscreen. Clothes that cover your skin will help keep you safe, too. It is also a good idea to wear a hat. Sunglasses can keep your eyes safe. It is important to keep both yourself and the ozone layer safe!

GLOSSARY

aerosol (ER-uh-sol) Something sprayed from a container in a fine mist.

atmosphere (AT-muh-sfeer) The gases around an object in space.

cells (SELZ) The basic units of living things.

chemicals (KEH-mih-kulz) Matter that can be mixed with other matter to cause changes.

chlorine (KLOR-een) A greenish yellow gas.

chlorofluorocarbons (klor-oh-flor-oh-KAHR-bunz) Chemicals that have carbon, chlorine, and fluorine in them.

environment (en-VY-ern-ment) Everything that surrounds people and other living things and everything that makes it possible for them to live.

oxygen (OK-sih-jen) A gas that has no color or taste and is necessary for people and animals to breathe.

ozone (OH-zohn) A gas that forms from oxygen.

ozone layer (OH-zohn LAY-er) A part of Earth's atmosphere.

satellites (SA-tih-lyts) Machines in space that circle Earth.

skin cancer (SKIN KANT-ser) A sickness in which skin cells grow too quickly.

ultraviolet ray (ul-truh-VY-uh-let RAY) A ray given off by the Sun that can hurt your skin and eyes.

INDEX

WEB SITES

Due to the changing nature of Internet links, PowerKids Press has developed an online list of Web sites related to the subject of this book. This site is updated regularly. Please use this link to access the list:
www.powerkidslinks.com/pop/ozone/